The Gospel Tract

The Power of the Gospel of Jesus Christ

by

Robert Alan Kosharek

For I am not ashamed of the gospel of Christ; for it is the power of God unto salvation... -- Romans 1:16a

The Gospel Tract

by Robert Alan Kosharek

Written 2004, published 2011

All Scripture taken from
the Authorized King James Bible,
God's perfect and preserved Word.

No Copyright for Jesus said,
"...freely ye have received, freely give"
-- Matthew 10:8.
Please include the entire page on any reproduction,
including the footer.

Scripture quotations from the Authorized King James Bible
need no permission to quote, print, or teach,
for the Word of God is not bound (2 Timothy 2:9).

ISBN-13: 978-0-9700193-2-5

Self-published using a Fellowes TB250 thermal binder
and supplies from www.mybinding.com.

The Gospel Tract

by Robert Alan Kosharek

"For the gospel is the power of God unto salvation." -- Romans 1:16

Preface

Where has the gospel gone? Where has the law gone in evangelism? Can we preach grace without law? Can we talk about the cross which reveals the magnitude of Christ's triumph over death without the law that shows us the depths of our sin?

Have we let the ever-changing culture define and redefine our witnessing? Do we look to 'strategies', 'new things', 'marketing', and entertainment as vehicles for the message we convey to the lost? Has political correctness watered down the gospel we 'preach'?

Have we discarded the 'key' to evangelism that Jesus taught?

Do we need to look beyond what God has provided us in the Scriptures to witness effectively?

In short, have we lost faith in the gospel of Jesus Christ which is the power of God unto salvation?

Acknowledgments

To God my savior for salvation, grace, love, and faith, in Whom I live, move, and have my being (Jude 3, Acts 17:28).

To my wife Mary Jean whose price is far above rubies (Pr 31:10-11) and in whom I have found a good thing (Pr 18:22).

To my sisters, Kathie and Judy, who faithfully prayed earnestly for my salvation (James 5:16b).

To the ministry of Ray Comfort at www.livingwaters.com who God is using to return the church to biblical evangelism.

Darkness

There is a way that seems right to man, but the end thereof is death. -- Proverbs 14:12

Andrew Walker, after running five blocks to catch the bus, walked to the last row and sat down, to catch his breath. It was his senior year and he couldn't afford to be late today for his final Physics exam. He started to relax. He was confident that job offers would come since he placed in the top fifth of his class. His self-assured smile beamed as he was confident that he would place first in this exam, and why not? Andrew had mastered the material and knew he deserved to. He had already done so on the previous two. He had found out early in life that he had a very orderly and logical mind, and enjoyed thinking, studying, absorbing, and learning. He not only enjoyed it; he thrived on it. He would take his studies way beyond their purpose and come to a much deeper understanding. So excelling on exams came fairly easily.

He reflected on the job interviews that would come. He relished the thought of having several firms bidding for his services. He smiled as he devised a way to work that to his advantage. He closed his eyes and rested his head against the bench seat.

"Hi. Do you know Jesus?!"

Andrew lifted his head and opened his eyes. Standing before him was an open-eyed, grinning teenager, looking like he was greeting his best friend. "Huh?" Andrew replied.

"Do you know Jesus Christ as your Savior? God says today is the day of salvation!" he bubbled back at Andrew.

"Say what?" Andrew asked quizzically. He ran his hand through his blond hair, pulling it up out of his eyes. It framed his face well and complemented his strong jawline.

The teenager sat down beside him and continued, "Yeah! God wants you to go to heaven- He loves you- that's why Jesus died on the cross! All you have to do is admit you've sinned and ask Jesus into your heart. What do you say?"

"Say to what?!"

"Say to going to heaven! Only God can fill that god-shaped vacuum in your heart!"

God-shaped vacuum? Andrew thought to himself- *what in the world is that?* Andrew had no such vacuum in his heart- he had a good heart- an awesome, life-pumping, enthusiastic heart, in fact. He had heard about God and all that Jesus stuff but somehow it never seemed real to him- just like any other religious story he had heard throughout his twenty years of life. He had learned a lot about the world in his four years in college and nothing seemed to indicate any truthfulness to the claims of this religion called 'Christianity'. He knew about their beliefs in a heaven and hell but just couldn't quite understand what they were talking about. To him that proved it wasn't true if he couldn't understand it- after all, he was acing some of the toughest exams in biophysics, one of the most demanding areas of science. If his intelligent mind could handle subjects that most of the world couldn't then certainly if heaven and hell were real he could understand it (1 Cor 2:14). "I don't have a god-shaped vacuum in my life."

The youngster hesitated briefly, "Yes you do!"

Andrew opened his eyes in disbelief, "I do?"

"Yes, you do- God says so," he replied earnestly.

"Really? Well, God must be mistaken because I haven't seen it!"

The teenager's shoulders drooped. He pleaded, not knowing what else to say, "Are you sure?"

"Yup!" Andrew said as he watched him turn to walk away.

The teenager shook his head as he walked away- for the life of him he couldn't figure out why anyone wouldn't want to believe in Jesus and go to heaven- *all it takes is a simple prayer!* He was dismayed when people refused his offer[1].

Andrew shook his head too- *what's that dude thinking? Just by repeating some silly prayer I'll go to heaven? That's all it takes? I could repeat his prayer without knowing what I was asking for!* To Andrew that didn't make

---

1 This young man has godly zeal and love for the lost, but failed to preach the gospel.

any sense at all. In truth, however, a part of Andrew had not been addressed; it lay dormant, after years of neglect. He spent the rest of the ride to campus staring out the window enjoying the sunny day.

The bus pulled to its stop at Downer and Kendall. Andrew got off and started his walk across campus to his physics class. Andrew felt at home here- it was here at college that he had developed from a boy into a man. He had been eager to learn about the world and his place in it. To learn about life and find out what it was that he wanted to do with it. After four immensely fulfilling years he not only had a 'well-rounded' education as they would say, but he had felt equipped to not only succeed in life, but to do it exceedingly well!

It started in his freshman year when he came across a campus magazine ad for Mensa, a society of intellectuals, entitled 'Take this I.Q. Test and Win a Color TV!' Andrew was curious so he took it. He mailed it in and found to his amazement that he scored ninety-three. Mensa contacted him and he took a supervised test and scored ninety-six; just two percent shy of qualifying for membership. That was the start; the catalyst which propelled Andrew Walker into his relentless personal quest for knowledge and truth. His thirst for knowledge was insatiable; it went far beyond a college education and specializing in biophysics. It included all aspects of life and the campus library that was more than adequate to accommodate him.

He strode leisurely across the square, enjoying the diversity of students- to him it represented the many different beliefs of life and reality. He had stopped often during these last four years discussing many philosophies which enriched his mind and made him a more rounded person, becoming wise in the ways of this world.[2] He walked past a row of booths set up by different student groups. As

---

2   This is exactly the same as during Paul's day in Acts 17:17 and 17:21. People came to the public square daily, discussing things and searching for some 'new' thing. 'New' things come and go- but sin hasn't and neither has how we are to preach the gospel. Paul preached by beginning with things of the natural world that they understood (17:22-23) and then swung the conversation of the spiritual (17:24-31). The gospel is timeless and needs no alteration in its presentation to the lost.

he walked by the Christian group he shook his head. He remembered his many debates, or rather heated arguments, with this extreme religious bunch. He couldn't believe the audacity of their claims that Christianity was the only true religion and the only way to heaven; if indeed there is a heaven. He kept walking.

Lost

No man can come to me, except the Father which hath sent me draw him:
and I will raise him up at the last day. -- John 6:44

"Excuse me, do you have a moment to answer a simple question?"

"Huh?" Andrew turned to his right and saw a simply radiant brunette with a huge smile catching up with him. "Yeah, sure, I guess," he replied and stopped and turned to face her. She continued, "If you died tonight and stood before God, and He asked you, 'Why should I let you into My heaven?' what would you say?"

That was a new one for Andrew- he had heard a lot of their preaching, but this was certainly a new angle. Since she was a babe he decided to engage her question. "Well, I guess I would say, 'Because you're a good God and a forgiving God You'll let me in'."

"So just by asking, you believe God will let you into heaven?"

"Yeah, I mean- that's the prayer, isn't it? A simple prayer asking God. Er, what's your name?" Andrew flashed a smile at her, hoping to get a reaction.

"Susan. Now back to the question" she said without any hint of a reaction, "Yes; Jesus said, 'Whoever calls upon the name of the Lord shall be saved.'"

Andrew thought that over a bit and replied, "Yup. I did that five years ago, so I'm a Christian and I'm going to heaven."

"But you don't go to church, and you still belong to that raunchy fraternity, Andrew. God wants you to give that stuff up and follow Jesus."

"And exactly how do you know I don't go to church? We're strangers, Susan," Andrew said surprised.

Susan hesitated, knowing Andrew's apartment neighbor Mark told her he doesn't go to church. She softened her remark, "well, how about that fraternity? Do you think God approves of that?"

"No, no- I want you to answer my question- how do you know I don't attend church?" Andrew asked directly. He wanted to know how a complete stranger knew his Sunday habits.

Susan again hesitated, knowing she had made a mistake- *forgive me, Lord- give me the words to say.* "Well, your neighbor Mark told me- he just happened to mention it casually as we were praying for students on campus."

"So you're little group is spying on me, hey? Mark is the plant- questioning me all the time to get the scoop, and then you guys pray in secret for me to join your little religious group. Man, that takes the cake! I'm doing just fine in life; a lot better than your sorry group- why don't you just worry about your own lives and leave the rest of us alone?" Andrew spouted.

"I'm sorry, Andrew. We just want to see you go to heaven! Can't you see that? Jesus came to save sinners."

"So now I'm a *sinner*? First you spy on me behind my back, then you judge my character? Susan, we don't even know each other- I know absolutely nothing about and would never claim to judge you- how in the world can you judge me?" he replied a bit heated at her insinuation that he was a sinner- she didn't even know him.

Susan saw she created a mess. "I'm sorry, Andrew- I'm sorry!" she said earnestly.

"Apology accepted. Just for the record, like I told you, I prayed the prayer. But I've learned a lot since then and I'm wiser and I know the world better. I know there's other truth out there and it has served me quite well. When I prayed that prayer years ago nothing happened. According to you Christians my life was supposed to change- 'an abundant life', right, Susan? Well guess what- it never happened. Instead my parents hated me and disowned me (Mat 10:35)- they thought I was in some cult. Two of my best friends taunted me, ridiculed me, and then stopped associating with me- said it would ruin their image (2 Tim 3:12)[3]. I went to a few fellowship meetings and went to church for awhile but I really didn't feel like it was for me- I didn't experience any abundant life; in fact it got worse.

---

3   Andrew receive persecution when he was promised an 'abundant life'- Yea, and all that will live godly in Christ Jesus shall suffer persecution.

Then I came to this college and I *pursued* life and I *found* it! I've *got* an abundant life!" (1 John 2:19)[4]

Susan was taken aback at his response- she had nothing to say in response; she was in fact confused as to why God hadn't changed his life after he prayed.

Meanwhile, Bill, who was listening from the group, joined them after hearing Andrew raising his voice. He walked over and calmly said, "you have to do more than just ask Him- you have to admit that you're a sinner and that you need Jesus Christ as your Savior."

"Oh, yeah- I'm a sinner- a huge, big, rotten sinner! Here come the righteous preaching! I'm going to hell if I don't confess- 'turn or burn', right, Susan?" He felt offended by their accusation.

"That's right. The Bible says 'all have sinned and fallen short of the glory of God'" (Ro 3:23[5]).

"So you're calling me a sinner, right? You self-righteous hypocrite! I heard about a couple of you Christians getting caught on your finals last year! Don't tell me about sin when you guys are full of it!" It was true; several of their group had been caught cheating on their exams.

Bill was hoping Andrew didn't know that- now the group's testimony was tainted and it was hurting his witness today (Mat 5:16[6]). "That's true; but they've since repented. But that doesn't change the fact that we're all sinners and need Christ as Savior."

"So? You sin and then you're sorry. Well, I do the same thing; I mess up and I apologize to those I've hurt- same thing. Plus, I prayed your prayer so according to you I'm already going to heaven- have a

---

4   Here's an example of a person who thinks he was saved, but wasn't because he wasn't preached the gospel and hadn't repented. He tries to live the Christian life and can't because he was never born again, hence he falls away and becomes more bitter than before because of the way he's treated by the world- They went out from us, but they were not of us; for if they had been of us, they would no doubt have continued with us: but they went out, that they might be made manifest that they were not all of us.

5   Not one ever lived a sinless life except Jesus Christ- For all have sinned, and come short of the glory of God.

6   Bill wanted their lives to shine of Christ to the lost that they may be saved- Let your light so shine before men, that they may see your good works, and glorify your Father which is in heaven.

nice day." And with that Andrew stomped off, infuriated and offended at them calling him a sinner without them ever knowing Andrew. His thoughts about asking Susan out had quickly vanished.

Bill turned and yelled after Andrew, "Jesus Christ is the way, the life, and the truth, Andrew!" (John 14:6)

Foolishness! (1 Cor 1:18[7]) Andrew thought to himself- *I'm a good person; I'm sorry for hurting others; I apologize;* (Pr 20:6[8]) *I prayed their prayer- if there's any truth to it then I'm going to heaven.* Again, that part of Andrew still had not been addressed; it still lay dormant, after years of neglect.

Back at the booth Susan and Bill could only shake their heads in exasperation, wondering why a man as smart as Andrew couldn't understand salvation and his need for Christ. "I just can't talk to him- he keeps coming up with something to refute whatever I try to tell him," Susan explained to Bill, "He's just so smart- he's always got some new question. I just wish for once I could say something to stop his mouth- to make him realize he doesn't know it all!" (Ro 3:19[9]) Bill shook his head in agreement, unable to add anything.[10]

Meanwhile, God was drawing Andrew unto Himself. (John 6:44)

---

7 The gospel was foolish to Andrew because he didn't yet know of his true state before God- For the preaching of the cross is to them that perish foolishness.

8 People think they're good and will tell you so- Most men will proclaim every one his own goodness.

9 There is something we can inform the lost of that will stop their mouths- Now we know that what things soever the law saith, it saith to them who are under the law: that every mouth may be stopped, and all the world may become guilty before God

10 Susan and Bill are dismayed at why Andrew doesn't understand; they too hadn't preached the gospel to Andrew.

Drawing

By the time he reached the physics building he felt better. He had calmed himself down by recalling all the truth he had learned; truth he could touch, feel, and experience- not this superstitious, mythological stuff that made no sense to his reasoning mind. Not once had any Christian been able to answer his questions about Christianity to his satisfaction; he was just too smart for them. They didn't have answers.

Just last year he heard some other Christians from the same group ranting on about, "God is love! God is love! Accept His free gift of grace in Jesus Christ!" He remembered them quoting John 3:16, "For God so loved the world that He sent his only begotten Son that whosoever should believe on him shall have everlasting life." *If God is love why would He send anyone to hell?* How's that for a paradox Andrew thought to himself. He was just thankful that he wasn't a religious person. *Foolishness!*

He pulled open the door to his lab and took his seat. Several students turned and smiled; others looked forward to Andrew acing the final. They knew he had a great chance to ace it- the last of three exams. And why not? He had solved the semester-long challenge from the professor early on; that made this 30-year professor take notice of Andrew. And now Andrew was about to do what had never been done before in Mr. Schermer's physics class- ace all three exams- his moment of glory had come.

It was a grueling exam, yet nevertheless, Andrew's intelligence and study overcame the tough exam. He was surprised at how hard Mr. Schermer had made it, but he would expect nothing less from the professor. It took him almost the entire period, but he used the extra time to ensure he had the correct answers for the tough parts. Above all else, he needed to feel completely sure of his answers. His passion to ace these three exams. His intelligence, along with his determination, would ensure a long and fruitful career as a biophysicist.

"Well, that's a first. You taking the entire two hours to finish the exam! Andrew, are you slipping?" Angela teased as she walked out with Andrew.

Andrew flashed a smile at her, enjoying the flirting, "I was distracted by your beauty, my dear."

"Oh, I see!" Angela replied, blushing. She'd be on cloud nine if he'd ask her out, "well, thanks! I look forward to the next chance I get to distract you." She knew he'd ask her out. She was the 'babe' of the class and made sure everyone knew it, especially Andrew. This was her chance, he would be hers.

"How about tonight? There's one of those outdoor jazz concerts at the union pavilion. I'd love to be distracted by you again." He knew she'd say yes- he could tell. He had dazzled her, as well as the rest of the class during lecture discussions. Even Mr. Schermer had been duly impressed. So he knew she would fall for him; probably quite hard- and she would be his.

"Well... I suppose," she replied hesitantly, not wanting to appear too eager, "Only if you get me back to my dorm by ten- I've still got one more exam tomorrow."

"Sounds great! I'll swing by to pick you up around six- OK?"

"Fine!"

"Great- see you then!" The two of them departed, both dreaming about each other and the night's date.

Fire and Brimstone

Andrew had a couple of hours before his bus came so he headed off to his fraternity. He walked a couple of blocks through the urban neighborhood that his college was nestled in, admiring the architecture of the nearly two-hundred year old buildings. This was one of America's oldest and revered universities. Andrew appreciated the history and prestige that was here. He took in the beautiful and elaborate landscaping that enhanced the antiquity of the surroundings. Mighty oaks lined the roads, presenting a huge shield to the sun's bright rays, that quickly turned the bright sunny avenue into a shadowed, cool stretch. His eyes took a few moments to adjust.

"Repent! Repent, I say! As John the Baptist came preaching the kingdom of heaven, so say I, repent!" came the booming voice over Andrew's right shoulder. Mason McCallister was at it again-bellowing out the old fire-and-brimstone preaching. He had done this every first Tuesday of the month. Since Andrew was in no hurry, he stopped to enjoy this guy's act. He sat down in the cool grass, pulling his knees up to his chin and wrapping his arms around them. He smiled as he looked up at Mason, ranting and raving.

"As did Pharaoh and the Egyptians drown in the red sea, so shall every man and woman today who doesn't turn to the almighty, wrath-filled God of vengeance! He will pour out His cup of wrath upon all the condemned of the world! Repent! Repent while the Lord offers salvation- for there will come a time when the offer will be withdrawn!" Mason rambled on, full of passion and seriousness. As he raved, he would pan the audience, which included no more than twenty students, with his intense, penetrating eyes, locking on to the unsuspecting, trying desperately to elicit the fear of the Lord.

His gaze fell upon a female sophomore. She was helpless to turn away- her eyes became big and her chin trembled. Andrew felt sorry for her. "Hey, excuse me..." Andrew waited until she could pull herself away from Mason's gaze. She turned to the voice next to her. "Do you have the time?" Andrew asked calmly.

"Time? Oh, ah... it's a little after one-thirty," she offered timidly and a little bit shaken.

"Thanks. Hey, don't listen to him- he's talking nonsense," Andrew assured her, "he comes out here every month spewing the same old trash. God loves you- He loves everybody- He would never send anybody to hell."

She smiled slightly at his comforting words. She was really wondering if it was true- if God was wanting her to repent- she certainly was fearful to an extent. *But,* she thought, *it would be hard to turn to this angry God! Besides, am I really that bad?*

"Hey, if this guy really was God's spokesman, would he come at you like a hell-bent, doom-and-gloom, raging preacher?" Andrew asked while making a overly-silly caricature of Mason's face.

"No, I guess not," she smiled again. She started to settle down.

"Good! That's good! Well, I've got to go. Have a good day. Enjoy the sun and forget this raving lunatic," Andrew suggested.

She smiled again and nodded her head. Andrew stood and walked off, shaking his head at all the religious nuts in the world.[11]

---

11 Here we have a man trying to convince others that they are sinners by *telling* them they are- this is offensive to the lost because they haven't *become convinced* that they truly are sinners. He failed to use the 'key' that Jesus talked about in Luke 11:52.

The Wisdom of the World

He headed into the local bookstore at the end of the block to pick up a couple of books he had been searching for. It was a quaint old shop, run by Harold Zifimeyer, an equally quaint and eccentric owner. He really appreciated that Andrew had formed a friendship with him the first time he came in looking for a copy of *The Mind Within*. He said "I don't have it, but if there's a copy in print, I'll find it!" True to his word, he called Andrew three months later when he secured a copy from a contact he had in Boston.

"Hey, Harold, how are you?" Andrew asked as he sped down the aisle towards the pick-up bin.

"Just fine, Andrew, and yourself?" Harold replied, pushing his glasses up on his forehead. His bushy, frizzy tufts of remaining silver hair made a convenient perch for the wire rims. He scuttled along into the back room, remembering that he always kept Andrew's books in the back- they were far too valuable to just leave lying in the pick-up bin out in the open. "Over here, Andrew, over here."

"Wonderful, wonderful," Andrew said as he turned back to see Harold lifting up in the air in triumph his latest find.

"Got it! A rare 1806 original copy of *Religion, Philosophy, & the Dawn of Relativism*." Harold exclaimed.

"Well, I'll be, Harold. I didn't think you'd come through this time- but if anyone could, it'd be you!"

"Ah, that's what I like to hear my boy!" Harold announced as he set it on the counter. Andrew got in line to pay for it and waited.

There was quite a line due to the popular once-a-year-sale Harold was having. It moved slowly. After a few minutes the guy two ahead of Andrew turned around to the lady ahead of Andrew and commented what a great sale it was. She agreed with him. He then asked her, "Say, haven't we met before somewhere on campus?"

She looked him over, trying to place him, "Not that I'm aware of."

"Oh, OK- case of mistaken identity he said with a smile. "By the way, isn't it great to have friends?"

She thought the comment a bit unusual, "Yeah- It sure is."

The man smiled even more and gladly offered, "So, how would you like to have Jesus for a friend?"

"Excuse me?" she said, taken aback.

"I said, *wouldn't you like to have Jesus for a friend?* You know, He's the best friend of all- He'll never leave you or forsake you!"

Andrew watched as the two of them chatted. She thought it over, "Well, what do I have to do to make Him my friend?"

"Just ask Him- say, Jesus, I'd like You for a friend! That's all there's is to it!"

"Seems rather harmless... OK, Jesus, will You be my friend?"

"Hey, that's great! He's your friend now! Isn't that great?"

"Sure, OK, I guess it is!" she beamed. She thought about it some more and felt really good inside. The guy gave her the thumbs up and turned forward again.

Andrew shook his head as he waited patiently in line.[12]

"Hello, just the one book today?" the cheery cashier asked Andrew as he approached the register.

"Yeah, that's it," Andrew replied with a smile of his own.

"Oh- this is that rare one Mr. Zifimeyer spent weeks trying to secure- looks like your the lucky recipient of his efforts," she mentioned as she rang it up. She was glad to have something nice to say to this customer- it was her goal to show the love of Jesus to every stranger she met. She had hoped that each customer would see Jesus in her.

"Yes- it is quite rare, but Mr. Zifimeyer's the best at locating them! Do you have any idea what this book is about?" he asked. He appreciated her friendliness.

She glanced at the title, *Religion, Philosophy, & the Dawn of Relativism.* "No, not really. But I hope you enjoy it- if you don't, you know you can return it for a full refund! We wouldn't want any customer to be unhappy with their purchase!" She seemed proud of the store's policy

---

12 This sincere Christian is witnessing from a book he read that actually says to just ask Jesus to be your friend and you'll become a Christian.

on returns. She became bold enough to add, "We believe in the golden rule- that's where that policy came from." She didn't want to sound religious or pushy and hoped that he would understand what she was saying.

"Oh, that's nice," Andrew replied as pulled out his wallet.

"Oh- say, there's a half-off sale today. If you buy one book at full price you get the second book at half-price. Were there any other books you were considering?"

Andrew thought for a moment. "No, but thanks for asking."

Another smile lit up her face, "No problem; just wanted to be of help."

Andrew returned the smile as he reached for a twenty. He handed it to her and she took it and started to place it in the till. As she did she saw two edges to the bill. She rubbed her fingers and discovered another twenty stuck to the first one. "Oh my- you gave me two twenties by mistake! Here's your extra one!"

"Oh, wow! Thanks!" Andrew said as he placed it back into his wallet.

"No problem!" she announced as she handed him his change.

"Thanks; have a good day," Andrew said as he grabbed the bag.

"Sure; you too!" she said cheerfully.

Andrew turned and headed for the door. *She's pretty nice. See, there's more proof that people are good. There's no way every person is 'bad' like some Christians keep harping about.*

As she waited on the next customer in line she thought *I hope he had a chance to see Jesus in me!*[13]

Andrew took the bus home thinking about the day's events. He

---

13 This is commonly called lifestyle evangelism. It's good to let your light so shine before men that they see your good works that glorify God, however, the lost will not make that connection between a Christian's godly behavior and Christianity unless they *tell them*. Andrew innocently concludes that she is a good person by nature because she failed to preach to him. Not wanting to sound 'religious' or 'preachy' Andrew is denied hearing the gospel, which is the power of God unto salvation.

had accomplished what he wanted- acing the exam. It hadn't been scored yet but he was confident. And Angela, wow! That was another achievement! Two-for-two today! No, wait a minute- actually he was three-for-three; the group of Christians on the campus square- he had won that debate too! He smiled in his victories; savoring them, imagining the success that was his. He reminisced over his dominant college years and his successes along the way- along with the struggles and challenges that life gives. He recalled various troubles he had and how he dealt with them. He smiled to himself, confident and content that he had what was necessary to succeed.

He jumped off at his stop and walked the four blocks to his apartment. He checked his mail and bounded up the steps to his second-story loft. As he turned the corner in the hall he spotted his neighbor Mark. "Hey, Mark- what's going on?"

"Hi, Andrew. Just another joyful day at work! How about you? Wasn't your big exam today? How did you do?"

"Great! Just great!" Andrew beamed.

"That's awesome, Andrew! God surely has blessed you!"

"Yeah, right, Mark," Andrew replied, doubting his claim, "have a good evening."

"You too, Andrew. Andrew?..." Mark said and then paused. *Oh oh, here it comes,* Andrew thought, *Mark's going to give his testimony again and ask me to be a Christian.*

"Have you ever thought where your intelligence comes from? Have you ever thought about God? Have you ever realized that you're lost without Him? I've got a tract I'd like to give you- will you read it?" He handed Andrew the Bridge tract.

"Sure, Mark, I'll read it," Andrew replied in defeat. He had previously adamantly opposed Mark but thought he'd finally take it and read it to get him off his back. *He's always preaching at me!* "Thanks, Mark. I'll read it."

"Great! I'll pray for you too!"

"Thanks," Andrew said as he opened his door and closed it behind him.

Mark closed his door. His roommate heard the conversation and asked Mark in frustration, "Why do you bother anymore? You know Andrew- if anyone's a lost cause, he is."

Mark sighed, "I know, Jim, I know," he said as he shook his head. His weariness got the better of him as he replied, "maybe you're right, Jim."

Meanwhile the heavens thundered with the awesome truth- *God is not slack concerning His promise... but is longsuffering toward us, not willing that any should perish, but that all should come to repentance* (2 Peter 3:9).

People Perish

My people perish for lack of the knowledge of the law. -- Hosea 4:6

Andrew tossed the tract on the kitchen table as he opened the refrigerator door looking for something to eat. He grabbed last night's leftovers and sat himself down at the table and started devouring. He usually gobbled down his meals at the kitchen table, and today was not any different. His eyes fell on the tract and his curiosity got him to pick it up and read it. It presented the "Roman Road" plan of salvation. It explained about how man is lost due to his sin and how Jesus Christ is the bridge back to God. It showed how man tries other ways to try to bridge that gap- good deeds, giving money, going to church, etc., but Jesus Christ is the only payment God will accept to get one to heaven.[14] *Interesting philosophy*, Andrew thought, *If I ever feel I need Jesus, I'll call on him. I'm a good person; sure I've done some wrong things, but no way am I a sinner like what this booklet is talking about- that's for the murderers and rapists, and spies who commit treason. I do a lot of good things- but who cares? None of this is real anyway.*[15]

With that he tossed the tract in the garbage with the remains of his meal. He let out a hearty burp which confirmed the tastiness of his meal, and then headed to the bathroom to prepare for his hot date

---

14 The Roman Road is biblical, yet it doesn't personally apply the gospel to its reader- the reader must *experience* the gospel instead of being given an *explanation*, since they can't discern spiritual things.

15 Galatians 2:21 I do not frustrate the grace of God: for if righteousness come by the law, then Christ is dead in vain. Good works don't please God- He does NOT accept one's good works- they're trying to bribe God due to their guilt. Romans 8:8 says the lost cannot please God: So then they that are in the flesh cannot please God. Why? Because they're an enemy of God- Romans 8:7 Because the carnal mind is enmity against God.

tonight.

After he showered and decided what to wear, he went through his positive affirmations, powerfully affirming them out loud. He read his goals list for the year and focused on the personal one about meeting someone special. His past success in doing this confirmed their truthfulness- it had brought him success beyond what he thought possible since graduating from high school. *Christians have their abundant life; I've got my awesome life!*

Then he cranked some of his favorite rock songs that always gave him confidence and power. He had a special tape made up of his favorites- ones that spoke directly to his needs and how to have the proper mental state of mind. Through the sheer emotional impact the music had on his attitude he found power, confidence, contentment, sympathy, and a host of other emotional states he could benefit from.

Lastly, he went through his success list- a list he made of all his accomplishments. This gave him great confidence in himself and the validity of his sources of knowledge; it confirmed him that he was on the right path and knew what life was all about- he was overwhelmingly happy, intelligent, popular, successful, compassionate, soon to be financially secure at the ripe old age of twenty-three, and after tonight, he would be enjoying a relationship with that someone special.

Angela was also preparing for her big date. She had dated a lot of guys on campus, but to land Andrew would be simply dreamy! She would be the envy of all her friends! And why not? Was she not the most popular? The most charming? The most beautiful? The most friendly? Didn't she work just as hard at achieving her dreams as Andrew did? Didn't she accomplish just as much within her circle of influence as Andrew? Of course she was worthy of him. Her college education had taught her that much- be your own woman- pursue your own dreams- get that successful career to prove your worthiness to society. Tonight would be her crowning achievement!

Twenty minutes later her dorm doorbell rang. It was Andrew. "Hi, beautiful!" he sang romantically as he thrust a bouquet of roses at her.

"Roses! Oh, Andrew! How romantic!" she explained with wide eyes. "I'm ready; lets go!"

"OK, we're off!" They walked out to his car; he opened the door for her. She got in and said thank you and off they drove to the pavilion.

They found a nice spot on the grass lawn in the middle with a direct view of the stage. Angela had decided to make a picnic out of it as she had laid down her blanket and pulled out her deluxe picnic basket- complete with snacks, wine, and place settings! They had arrived early and enjoyed the next hour getting to know each other better. Soon the lawn filled to capacity and the concert got underway. It was a very enjoyable evening- music to sooth the soul and pleasant weather to calm the nerves. Various food and drink vendors catering to the crowd's thirst while a few arts and crafts vendors had set up shop. People were milling around chatting with others. Andrew and Angela found themselves enjoying the music, the wine, the night, and each other quite a bit- it was going extremely well for both of them- romance was in the air.

Ninety-minutes later the jazz ensemble took a break. People got up to stretch, visit the restrooms, and walk around. Andrew and Angela preferred to spend the time people-watching. This was an ideal place to do it. These types of gathering always brought out various social groups of society- music seemed to bring everyone together. Andrew scanned the crowd. He noticed one young man who apparently was making the rounds to people handing out some type of pamphlet and then engaging them in conversation. (2 Tim 4:2 [16]) *I wonder what his cause is?* Angela spent her time noticing the different fashion statements people were making and wondered if they were trying to express themselves through dress. She tried to guess what types of personalities people had based upon how they dressed. The break soon ended and the concert resumed. The second set was better than the first- it really showcased the talent that this

---

16 2 Timothy 4:2 Preach the word; be instant in season, out of season.

up-and-coming ensemble had.

The Law of the Lord is perfect, converting the soul. -- Psalm 19:7

As the final break began Andrew turned his thoughts back to Angela after really getting into that last set. Angela had too apparently, for she hardly noticed Andrew. Andrew thought things were going really well- *that Angela is something special. I've really made an impression. Yes, success will be mine- Angela digs me!* He took great comfort in this, knowing he would once again succeed because he had learned so much and taken time to learn the ways of the world, and the promises it made to all. *Man, I've got it made! This is awesome! Life is awesome! I've got it made- first I ace the exams and then I meet Angela! His inner strength, conviction, and confidence took another huge leap forward. All I've learned and studied for is finally paying off!*

"Wow, that was great, wasn't it?" Angela beamed as she turned towards Andrew.

"Yes; they're quite good- I've got their latest CD," Andrew replied as his eyes twinkled. They spent the next few moments gazing at each other, then turned to watch the crowd once more. Andrew's hand slowly crept over to Angela's, and he placed it on top of hers, while looking the other way. Angela was surprised but kept her hand there, knowing Andrew had fallen for her.

"Excuse me, did you get one of these?" a man asked Andrew and Angela[17]. Andrew turned along with Angela to see a young man holding out a small card. Andrew reached out and instinctively took it, seeing that it was labeled *Intelligence Test*, and had five questions on the front.

"No, what is it?" Andrew asked out of curiosity.

"It's an intelligence test. Would you like to take it?"

Andrew's pride sparked as he let out a huge grin- so huge Angela couldn't miss it. Angela returned the smile thinking, *go ahead; take it;*

---

17 Adapted from the approach Jesus used as explained by Ray Comfort at www.wayofthemaster.com.

show him your genius! At first Andrew thought this guy was another one of those religious nuts pushing Jesus in his face, but apparently he was just out trying to help people enjoy the evening.

"Sure, I'll take it," he replied with interest.

"Good," the young man said. He crouched down and handed one to Angela too, so she could follow along. "OK, question number one. A lady read a book, turned the light out and went to sleep. In the morning, when she saw in the newspaper that a ship had sunk drowning all on board, she committed suicide. Why?"

Andrew thought intensely, as was his nature. *OK, OK, what clues do we have here?* He drew upon all his mental prowess, wanting both to solve the riddle and to impress Angela. *She committed suicide- why? What did she find out that caused her to take that action? She read the newspaper- a boat sank, people drowned. What did that have to do with her? Well, the last thing she did before going to bed was that she turned off the light. Now what kind of light must she have turned off to cause a boat to sink and all on board drown? Light, light- what's are various important types of lights; they must deal with the sea, since that's where the ship sunk... a lighthouse! That's it! She turned out the lighthouse searchlight- the ship didn't see it and crashed upon hitting the shore!* "She committed suicide because she was the lighthouse keeper!" Andrew gladly exclaimed.

"That's right!" the young man said in the same tone, "Good- you're a bright man! Are you ready for question two?"

"Yes!" Andrew said, really enjoying this. Angela smiled as well, reveling in Andrew's intelligence. The young man took him through three more questions then asked him the final one, "Do you think you're a good person?"

Andrew chuckled at this one, "Yes! I am a good person!" (Pr 20:6 [18])

"Would you like to find out if that's true?" the young man asked gently (2 Cor 5:11[19]).

---

18 Most men will proclaim every one his own goodness. Most people will say they're a good person- and why not? They've been told that all their life by family and friends. But that's according to man's standards and not God's- the Ten Commandments.

19 Knowing therefore the terror of the Lord, we persuade men. Believers know

"Sure!" Andrew was eagerly looking forward to answering yet another question.

"You've heard of the Ten Commandments, haven't you?"

"Yes, I have."

"How many can you name?"

"Ah, let's see... you shouldn't lie... steal... covet, eh, what else?... You shouldn't, eh, swear?"

"Right- take God's name in vain. So, have you ever told a lie?" (1 Timothy 1:8[20])

Andrew was taken back a bit by the unusual question, "Yes; I've told lies."

"So what does that make you?"

" A person who lies, I guess."

"But more specifically, what does that make you?" the young man said meekly.

"One who hasn't told the truth one-hundred percent of the time?" Andrew didn't understand what the young man was driving at.

"If I lied to you, what would you call me?" (Col 4:6[21])

"A liar. Oh, I get it- I'd be a liar; I get it."

"Right. Now... what's your name?"

"Andrew, and this is Angela."

Angela smiled and the young man turned and smiled at Angela. He turned back to Andrew, "Now, Andrew, have you ever stolen anything, regardless of value?"

"Yes, I have," Andrew said as something deep inside him stirred. Before he had a chance to engage his mind he heard...

"What does that make you?"

"A sinner," Andrew replied plainly.

"Yes, but more specifically- what does that make you?"

"A thief," Andrew replied plainly.

"Good- you're right again," The young man said in a sure, even

_____

what awaits the lost person when he dies, along with God's wrath, therefore we do what we can to persuade the lost.

20 But we know that the law is good, if a man use it lawfully.

21 Let your speech be alway with grace, seasoned with salt, that ye may know how ye ought to answer every man.

tone, looking right into Andrew's eyes. "Now, Jesus said, 'whoever looks with lust at a woman has already committed adultery with her in his heart.' Have you ever looked with lust at a woman?" (Matt 5:27-28[22])

Andrew's mind instantly flashed through many times he had done this, "Yes, I have." He was surprised that he said it for Angela was right next to him, yet he couldn't deny the truth of it; he had lusted after a woman; many women, in fact- even Angela...

"So what does that make you?"

Andrew began feeling knots in his stomach. He glanced down. This conversation was going somewhere he didn't know- and that made him feel uncomfortable. Again, he had the immediate knowledge that the answer was 'an adulterer'. *I'm an adulterer!* Andrew had just come to that truth. He plainly knew it beyond a doubt- his inner sense had just informed him that he was an adulterer- not only that, but he was a liar and a thief. It was not something that his intellect told him; it was not anything this young man was forcing upon him- indeed, he had merely asked him questions. No, this truth came from somewhere else. Some part of Andrew that had not been addressed; that had laid dormant, after years of neglect, had suddenly come alive- his *conscience*. (Ro 2:15[23])

Andrew faced a moment of truth; would he admit it to this stranger, or would he - for the first time he could remember - violate the obvious truth that he knew and always tried to honestly pursue and lie instead.

Andrew looked up at the young man and said plainly, almost weakly, "that makes me an adulterer." His mind started racing in frantic circles- that part of him that thirsted all of his life for the things of the world suddenly arose in fiery passion- he realized that it

---

22 Ye have heard that it was said by them of old time, Thou shalt not commit adultery: But I say unto you, That whosoever looketh on a woman to lust after her hath committed adultery with her already in his heart.

23 Andrew had a conscience given to him by God that he might know sin. Which shew the work of **the law written in their hearts**, their **conscience also bearing witness**, and their thoughts the mean while **accusing** or else excusing **one another**.

was running his life; and he would do anything to satisfy it- *sin*. It had been dead; now the Commandments began reviving it. (Ro 7:8-10[24]).

"OK, here's the last question- have you ever taken God's name in vain- you know, using it as a curse word?"

"Yes, I have; plenty of times," Andrew had to admit.

"So, Andrew," the young man spoke quietly, "you've taken the name of the God who has given you life, and used it as a curse word instead of using a four-letter word to express disgust. God calls that blasphemy." (Exodus 20:7[25]) Andrew swallowed hard. The young man didn't skip a beat; he lead right into his follow-up question, "So, Andrew, by your own admission, you're a lying, thieving, adulterer at heart, and you admit that you've blasphemed God. By that standard, the Ten Commandments, if you died tonight and stood before God on Judgment Day, would you be innocent or guilty?" (1 Timothy 1:8-9[26], (Ro 1:20[27])

Andrew knew the answer to that one, "I'd be guilty" came his automatic reply. His intellect had ceased. (Ro 3:19[28])

The young man continued in earnest, "Would you go to heaven or hell?" (1 Cor 6:9[29])

---

24 Without the law Andrew was dead to sin- he had no knowledge of it- once he heard it he *knew* he was a sinner. But sin, taking occasion by the commandment, wrought in me all manner of concupiscence. For without the law sin was dead. For I was alive without the law once: but when the commandment came, sin revived, and I died. And the commandment, which was ordained to life, I found to be unto death.

25   Thou shalt not take the name of the LORD thy God in vain; for the LORD will not hold him guiltless that taketh his name in vain.

26 The law is good since it brings a knowledge of sin that the person might know his need for Christ. But we know that **the law is good**, if a man use it lawfully; Knowing this, that **the law is** not made for a righteous man, but for the lawless and disobedient, for the ungodly and **for sinners**...

27 Andrew is without excuse- he is responsible for his sin. ...they are without excuse.

28 The law had done its work- Andrew couldn't say anything in reply- *his mouth was stopped*. Now we know that what things soever the law saith, it saith to them who are under the law: **that every mouth may be stopped**, and all the world may become guilty before God.

29 All unrepentant sinners will have their part in the lake of fire. Know ye not that the unrighteous shall not inherit the kingdom of God?

"I'd go to hell," Andrew answered matter-of-factly. Inwardly, he started to shutter; he had never before known such desperation- such finality. (Ro 6:23[30])

"Does that concern you?" (2 Cor 5:11[31])

Andrew drew a heavy, long sigh, "I guess it does." Fear started creeping up. (Pr 16:6[32])

"Good- it should, Andrew. You've broken God's law- the Ten Commandments. His wrath abides on you (John 3:36[33]); and He is angry with the wicked every day (Ps 7:11[34]). You're in big trouble, Andrew," he stated in earnest.

Andrew did not turn away from the young man's gaze- he couldn't- what could he do? He was guilty, and he knew it. He *had* broken God's laws- all ten of them; he *had* no excuse- he *was* guilty. He began to see the seriousness of his sin (Ro 7:13[35]). "I had no idea- I, I... I never really *knew* that I had *sinned*- holy cow, *there is a God!*" (Ro 7:11[36]) Andrew stammered as he started to turn pale.

"You've got an appointment with God one day, Andrew. You're going to die and then you'll face a holy God on the day of judgment (Heb 9:27[37]). Every day you continue in your sin you're storing up wrath for your day of judgment" (Ro 2:4[38]).

---

30 For the wages of sin is death.

31 Knowing therefore the terror of the Lord, we persuade men.

32 Fear causes sinners to flee from their sin. ...by the fear of the LORD men depart from evil.

33 God's wrath is on *every* lost person. ...he that believeth not the Son shall not see life; but the wrath of God abideth on him.

34 Why? Because God is holy and cannot tolerate sin. ...God is angry with the wicked every day.

35 The law was now doing its good work in Andrew- showing him the depth and depravity of his nature and his offense against God. ...that sin by the commandment might become exceeding sinful.

36 Sin, through the law, showed Andrew its deception. For sin, taking occasion by the commandment, deceived me, and by it slew me.

37 Andrew knew with certainty that the moment he dies he'd stand before God in judgment. And as it is appointed unto men once to die, but after this the judgment.

38 Andrew became aware that every time he sinned he was storing up wrath against himself. But after thy hardness and impenitent heart treasurest up unto thyself wrath against the day of wrath and revelation of the righteous

Andrew continued to hold his gaze, saying nothing. He felt faint inside; as he began to lose all the strength and vitality he had possessed. Yet he didn't dare turn away- he somehow knew he needed to hear this (Ps 51:6[39]).

"Andrew, it's a fearful thing to fall into the hands of the living God (Heb 10:31[40]). God commands you to repent because He has appointed a day in which He will judge the world in righteousness (Acts 17:30-31[41]).

Andrew couldn't take it- he was falling apart. All of his confidence and knowledge started falling away- it was useless- gaining him nothing (Pr 14:12[42]). He pleaded to the young man, "yeah, I think you're right- what can I do?" (Gal 3:24, Acts 2:37, 16:30[43])

"God is just and the penalty for sin must be paid, Andrew. Two-thousand years ago Jesus came down to earth as a man and paid your fine for you so you wouldn't have to spend eternity in hell. He lived the only sinless life. He was scourged, mocked, spit upon, and crucified. He died, was buried, and on the third day He rose again

---

judgment of God.

39 God wants man to know the truth. Behold, thou desirest truth in the inward parts: and in the hidden part thou shalt make me to know wisdom.

40 It is a fearful thing to fall into the hands of the living God.

41 And the times of this ignorance God winked at; but now commandeth all men every where to repent.

42 There is a way which seemeth right unto a man, but the end thereof are the ways of death.

43 The law now having done its work preparing the stony ground of Andrew's heart, he flees to the Savior. Gal 3:24 Wherefore **the law was our schoolmaster to bring us unto Christ**, that we might be justified by faith. Nothing has changed since Christ's day- sinful men will cry out today for the Savior when they realize their true state before a holy God. Acts 2:37 Now when they heard this, **they were pricked in their heart**, and said unto Peter and to the rest of the apostles, Men and brethren, **what shall we do?** And again in a different situation- Acts 16:30 And brought them out, and said, **Sirs, what must I do to be saved?**

according to the Scriptures[44]. Andrew, God loves you (John 3:16[45]) and He doesn't want you to go to hell (2 Peter 3:9[46]). Jesus took *all* of God's wrath on the cross for your sins and mine, and paid your entire debt in full- He exclaimed 'it is finished'" (John 19:30[47]). Something deep in Andrew flickered. The young man continued, *"you must repent*- that means turn from your sin- (Acts 2:38, 20:21, Luke 13:5[48]) and put your faith in Jesus Christ. God says *today* is the day of salvation (2 Cor 6:2[49]). Do you own a Bible?"

"Yes, I do," Andrew recalled when Mark had given him one last year. He had thrown it on the bottom shelf of his bookcase. He was surprised he still had it.

"Good. Go home, consider what God has said to you today, and *put on the Lord Jesus Christ*- that means to put your faith and trust in Him. You can't save yourself (Eph 2:8-10[50]). Turn from your sin and God will save you- He'll give you a new heart and a new spirit (Eze 36:26[51]). Read your Bible every day and obey what it says. God will never let you down."

---

44 **1 Cor 15:1-4** Moreover, brethren, I declare unto you the gospel which I preached unto you, which also ye have received, and wherein ye stand; By which also ye are saved, if ye keep in memory what I preached unto you, unless ye have believed in vain. For I delivered unto you first of all that which I also received, how that Christ died for our sins according to the scriptures; And that he was buried, and that he rose again the third day according to the scriptures:

45 For God so loved the world, that he gave his only begotten Son, that whosoever believeth in him should not perish, but have everlasting life.

46 The Lord is not slack concerning his promise, as some men count slackness; but is longsuffering to us-ward, not willing that any should perish, but that all should come to repentance.

47 When Jesus therefore had received the vinegar, he said, **It is finished**...

48 **Acts 2:38** Then Peter said unto them, **Repent**, and be baptized every one of you in the name of Jesus Christ for the remission of sins... **Acts 20:21** Testifying both to the Jews, and also to the Greeks, **repentance toward God**, and faith toward our Lord Jesus Christ. **Luke 13:5** I tell you, Nay: but, **except ye repent**, ye shall all likewise perish.

49 ...behold, now is the accepted time; behold, now is the day of salvation.

50 For **by grace** are ye saved through faith; and that **not of yourselves**: it is the gift of God: **Not of works**, lest any man should boast.

51 A new heart also will I give you, and a new spirit will I put within you: and I will take away the stony heart out of your flesh, and I will give you an heart of flesh.

"That sounds so simple," Andrew replied in amazement. (2 Cor 11:3b[52])

The young man smiled- for the first time. "Good. Thanks for listening." Andrew nodded silently. The young man stood and walked off. Andrew sat there for a few minutes while Angela looked away.

"I guess it's over," Andrew said glancing at the stage- the concert had ended.

"Yeah, you're right- it is over," Angela replied incredulous over what she had just witnessed, dropping her tract on the grass. She couldn't believe Andrew fell for this (Mark 4:5[53]). They drove home in silence; Andrew dropped her off without a word and continued home. He arrived home, slumping on his couch, falling into a desperate sleep.

---

52 ...the simplicity that is in Christ.
53 And some fell on stony ground, where it had not much earth. Andrea had a hardened heart, therefore she could not respond to the truth.

Preach the Word, In Season and Out of Season

And when he is come, he will reprove the world of sin, and of righteousness, and of judgment. John 16:8

He awoke at dawn to the brilliant light flooding his loft. He got up, took a shower, dressed, and prepared breakfast. As he ate, his mind was swimming with last night's stunning revelation. *Ah, that's all bogus!* He thrust the thought upon his consciousness. His mind subsided a bit, and he finished his breakfast. He decided to take a spin on his motorcycle- he needed to clear his head. He headed outside and revved her up. He took off, feeling the freedom of the breeze upon his face and the bright sun upon his skin. *Freedom! Escape!* He headed out to the country where the winding roads excited him as he rode out into the vast countryside.

He found a park and pulled over to stop. He spotted a picnic bench, sat down, pulled out his Gatorade and chugged it down. He leaned back and let out a big sigh. His mind calmed as he broke into his first smile of the day. In a moment he felt peace once again- everything was OK.

Then suddenly in the next moment the flood of thoughts returned- they broke upon him like a tidal wave (John 16:8[54]). One after one; then ten in a row; then hundreds- like gigantic waves pounding upon the shores of his soul.

Tears started flowing as Andrew broke down and started shaking. He felt disgusted at himself now knowing the depths of his sin (John 16:9[55])- he reviled himself- he had no righteousness of his own (Isaiah

---

54 And when he is come, he will reprove the world of sin, and of righteousness, and of judgment.
55 Of sin, because they believe not on me...

64:6[56])- his good deeds were worthless (John 16:10[57]). He feared the mighty judgment of God that he knew was coming (John 16:11[58]). His mind inundated him with the many, many, thousands of sins he had committed over his short twenty-two years- his lies, his adultery- both physical and imagined, his self-righteousness- thinking himself better than much of the world, his craving for money, his lust for success. Experience after experience of his blasphemy overtook him- he had cursed the God who gave him life. Fear of a holy God flooded him (Ps 90:11[59]). It continued on- memory after memory; sin after sin. The disrespect he gave his parents; the rebellion he lived to his elders and those in authority. The disdain he had for those less fortunate than himself. His awful, deceptive emotional life he lived through idolatry of rock music.

He saw clearly now that his every act was ultimately to serve himself (Eph 5:29[60]). He had no true love for his neighbor apart from it benefiting himself in the end.

Most importantly, he had forsaken the fist and greatest commandment, Thou shalt have no other gods before me (Ex 20:3). Andrew lived for himself alone, and not for God.

His soul groaned inside him (Psalm 32:3[61]); he felt a heavy hand upon him (Psalm 32:3[62]); his vitality drained out of him (Psalm 32:4[63]). He felt his life dissipating; slowly ebbing away- like an electronic toy whose batteries were quickly running low.

---

56 Isaiah 64:6 But we are all as an unclean thing, and our righteousness is as filthy rags; and we all do fade as a leaf; and our iniquities, like the wind, have taken us away.

57 ...Of righteousness, because I go to my Father, and ye see me no more...

58 ...Of judgment, because the prince of this world is judged...

59 Who knoweth the power of thine anger? even according to thy fear, so is thy wrath.

60 For no man ever yet hated his own flesh; but nourisheth and cherisheth it...

61 When I kept silence, my bones waxed old through my roaring all the day long.

62 For day and night thy hand was heavy upon me: my moisture is turned into the drought of summer.

63 I acknowledged my sin unto thee, and mine iniquity have I not hid. I said, I will confess my transgressions unto the LORD; and thou forgavest the iniquity of my sin.

Holy Spirit Conviction

For godly sorrow worketh repentance to salvation. 2 Corinthians 7:10a

It was at that moment that he felt a deep, penetrating sorrow over his sin (2 Cor 7:10[64]). It was as if he finally faced it and agreed with it- how could he not? This was truth; this was his life; this was Andrew Walker. He slumped, he gasped for air, he felt faint.

Inside, he gave up; he couldn't resist this awful conviction any longer. *I am a broken man.* "God, save me!" Andrew Walker cried out. Repentance from God had fallen upon him (2 Tim 2:25[65], Ro 2:4[66]). "Oh, Lord! Lord! Forgive me! Oh, God, forgive me!" he screamed as he convulsed (Psalm 32:5a[67]). He stumbled over and fell to the ground, lost in heavy, gut-wrenching convulsions, crying tears of sorrow.

Andrew Walker repented.

---

64 For godly sorrow worketh repentance to salvation...
65 ...if God peradventure will **give them repentance** to the acknowledging of the truth.
66 ...not knowing that **the goodness of God leadeth thee to repentance**?
67 **I acknowledged my sin unto thee**, and mine iniquity have I not hid.

Godly Sorrow Leads to Repentance

The Lord is not willing that any should perish... but that all should come to repentance. 2 Peter 3:9

In an instant of time, too small to measure, all of heaven rejoiced! The angels were overcome with joy! For a sinner had come to repentance! (Luke 15:10[68]) The everlasting heaven of God thundered in awesome praise to the glory of God! One of the greatest miracles of modern day had just been performed again by the mighty hand of God! Joy immeasurable pervaded all of the heavenly hosts. Another soul had been ransomed by the Lamb's blood from the bondage of the evil one, Satan! His name was found in the Book of Life! He was forever made secret in Christ and was instantly and forever seated in the heavenlies! (Eph 1:3[69])

In that instant of time Andrew Walker was converted. God forgave him his sins (Psalm 32:5b[70]). He had been translated from the kingdom of darkness into the kingdom of His dear Son (Col 1:13). The Holy Spirit regenerated him (Titus 3:5[71]); he passed from death unto eternal life (John 5:24[72]). He was born again (John 3:3[73]). Christ's

---

68 Likewise, I say unto you, there is joy in the presence of the angels of God over one sinner that **repenteth**.
69 Blessed be the God and Father of our Lord Jesus Christ, who hath blessed us with all spiritual blessings in heavenly places in Christ.
70 ...and thou forgavest the iniquity of my sin.
71 Not by works of righteousness which we have done, but according to his mercy he saved us, by the washing of regeneration, and renewing of the Holy Ghost.
72 Verily, verily, I say unto you, He that heareth my word, and believeth on him that sent me, hath everlasting life, and shall not come into condemnation; but is passed from death unto life.
73 Jesus answered and said unto him, Verily, verily, I say unto thee, Except a man be born again, he cannot see the kingdom of God.

righteousness was imputed to Andrew (James 2:23[74]); the wages of his sin paid; justice had been served (Ro 8:30[75]) and he was now a beloved child of God (1 John 3:1[76]), adopted of God (Gal 4:5[77]).

Andrew received a new heart and a new spirit (Eze 36:26). He was now a new creature in Christ Jesus (2 Cor 5:17[78]), and an ambassador for Christ (2 Cor 5:20[79]).

---

74 And the scripture was fulfilled which saith, Abraham believed God, and it was imputed unto him for righteousness: and he was called the Friend of God.
75 Moreover whom he did predestinate, them he also called: and whom he called, them he also justified: and whom he justified, them he also glorified.
76 Behold, what manner of love the Father hath bestowed upon us, that we should be called the sons of God: therefore the world knoweth us not, because it knew him not.
77 To redeem them that were under the law, that we might receive the adoption of sons.
78 Therefore if any man be in Christ, he is a new creature: old things are passed away; behold, all things are become new.
79 Now then we are ambassadors for Christ...

Conversion

*He brought me up also out of an horrible pit, out of the miry clay,
and set my feet upon a rock, and established my goings.
And he hath put a new song in my mouth, even praise unto our God:
many shall see it, and fear, and shall trust in the LORD.* Psalm 40:2-3

Several months later, rejoicing in his salvation, Andrew went out in search of the young man who preached the gospel of Jesus Christ to him. During those months Andrew had dug into the Bible reading and understanding whatever he could about God's gift of grace. He had wept many times with joy over the fact that he was truly forgiven, dead to sin, alive to Jesus, and forever destined for heaven! He still couldn't fathom God's love in the light of his sinful life. He kept shaking his head as he would read Romans chapter three and discover that *everyone* was a sinner, and then read chapter eight and see God's righteousness and love for everyone (Ro 5:8[80]). It was all he could think about- God's love and mercy for *him*. Romans 5:8 continually blew him away – *While we were yet sinners, Christ died for us.*

Every day his love and gratitude grew for God (1 John 3:1). He found a loving, Bible-based church and his heart would ache for righteousness during the service (Mat 5:6[81]). Many sinful habits dropped from his life (Ro 6:11[82]), and he truly enjoyed obeying whatever he found in the Bible as God enabled him (John 14:15[83]).

He checked out all the local parks. He scoured public events, praying mightily that he might catch up with this faithful servant of

---

80 But God commendeth his love toward us, in that, while we were yet sinners, Christ died for us.
81 Blessed are they which do hunger and thirst after righteousness: for they shall be filled.
82 Likewise reckon ye also yourselves to be dead indeed unto sin, but alive unto God through Jesus Christ our Lord.
83 If ye love me, keep my commandments.

God. After three weeks he found him, methodically working his way through a good-sized crowd at the opening of a new wing of the local museum.

Andrew waited for him to take a break and approached him as he sat down on a bench, placing his tracts next to him, sipping some water. Andrew asked hopefully, "excuse me, do you remember me?!"

The young man turned and looked at Andrew- no recollection showed on his face. Then it came to him- the man at the jazz concert, "ah, yes- I remember now. How are you? Did you give heed to God?"

"Yes! Yes, I did!" Andrew exclaimed, "the next day conviction fell and God saved me!"

The young man beamed with joy- (Pr 11:30[84]). He looked into Andrew's eyes and smiled. Andrew received the humble smile of love from his new brother in the Lord. They shared a moment of silent fellowship. Peace pervaded their souls as they sat in the sunshine of the day, rejoicing in the God of their salvation.

Andrew sat down on the bench next to him. "I... I can't tell you enough how grateful I am to you for preaching the gospel to me- I was lost and hopeless- and didn't even know it, yet now I see the power of the gospel that works salvation," Andrew said softly as tears formed.

"Yes, God's word will not return void," the young man replied. As they sat enjoying the joy of the Lord, a distinguished man in a double-breasted suit sat down on the other side of Andrew, his Wall Street Journal in hand. He nodded a 'good day' to Andrew and turned to his paper.

Andrew turned back to the young man and smiled as he grabbed a tract off the bench. Turning to the distinguished man he asked, "Excuse me, did you get one of these?"

---

84 ...he that winneth souls is wise.

Epilogue

Some time later Andrew met again with the young man. "So tell me," Andrew asked inquisitively, "how come I wasn't saved during any of those previous times when Christians witnessed to me?" Since Andrew's salvation his ever-alert and pondering mind couldn't help but wonder why God never saved him during any of those earlier times. He had hoped the young man could help.

"What did they say? What gospel did they preach to you?" the young man asked.

"One guy just came up to me excitedly telling me about Jesus and how He would fill the vacuum in my heart and give me a wonderful plan for my life. That made no sense to me since I already had a wonderful life- I didn't need or really want the life Jesus was supposedly offering."

"So how do we discern whether this is a correct way to witness or not?"

"I'm not completely sure- by the Bible?"

"Exactly- that is our duty before God. Let's see what God says. In the book of Acts there was a group of believers who lived in Berea who heard Paul and confirmed what he said by the Bible- '...they received the word with all readiness of mind, and searched the scriptures daily, whether those things were so.' (Acts 17:11). So God wants us to take everything we hear and confirm it against His Word. If it doesn't hold up then we are to reject it. Even if it is someone as mature and spiritual as the apostle Paul!

"God commands us to walk in truth- 'I rejoiced greatly that I found of thy children walking in truth, as we have received a commandment from the Father.' (2 John 3, 3 John 4). The word 'truth' is used 11 times in 2nd and 3rd John. We discern the truth by their doctrine- 'Whosoever transgresseth, and abideth not in the doctrine of Christ, hath not God. He that abideth in the doctrine of Christ, he hath both the Father and the Son. If there come any unto you, and bring not this doctrine, receive him not into *your* house, neither bid him God speed' (2 John 9-10). That's pretty clear- whoever doesn't hold to the doctrine of Jesus Christ we are to avoid.

"Notice the emphasis God puts on our responsibility to discern sound doctrine. Paul writes- urging us in this matter- to avoid things which are against doctrine, that some by their good words and fair speeches will deceive the simple, or those not mature in the faith- 'Now I beseech you, mark them that cause divisions and offences contrary to doctrine... and avoid them. ...by good words and fair speeches deceive the hearts of the simple.' (Ro 16:17-18). We are to hold fast to sound doctrine- 'Holding fast the faithful word as he hath been taught, that he may be able by sound doctrine both to exhort and convince the gainsayers.' (Titus 1:9). Believers are to ensure what we say is true- 'But speak thou the things which become sound doctrine.' (Titus 2:1).

"Why is doctrine so important? Because it guides us into the *truth*- and truth is paramount to God- Jesus said He is '...the way, *the truth, and the life*.' (John 14:6). The world is full of deception and God does not want us to go astray.

"Sound doctrine is essential also because deception is growing, and God tells us a great apostasy or falling away will occur- 'But know this, that in the last days perilous times will come. For men shall be lovers of own selves... lovers of pleasure more than lovers of God... having a form of godliness but denying the power thereof; from such turn away. Ever learning and never able to come to the knowledge of the truth' (2 Tim 3:1-2, 4-6). We have more Christian literature, books, and Internet resources than ever before yet God says apostasy is coming.

"Moreover, God says there will be many deceivers coming- 'for many deceivers are entered into the world...' (2 John 7); '...many false prophets shall come, and deceive many.' (Matt 21:11). Jesus warns us to take heed lest we be deceived- '...Take heed that no man deceive you.' (Matt 24:4). 'For the time will come when they will not endure sound doctrine... they shall turn away from the truth' (2 Tim 4:3-4).

"But by sound doctrine we will be able to know the truth and avoid deception- 'reprove, rebuke, exhort with all longsuffering and doctrine.' (2 Tim 4:2). God commands us to withdraw ourselves from those who don't have sound doctrine- 'If any man teach otherwise, and consent not to the wholesome words, even the words of our Lord Jesus Christ, and to the doctrine... he is proud, knowing nothing... from such withdraw thyself.' (1 Tim 6:3-5).

"How much untruth can we tolerate in someone's ministry? God says 'A little leaven leaveneth the whole lump' (Gal 5:9). I'll let the Holy Spirit give you the understanding in that."

Andrew's head started to swim- so much to learn; so much responsibility to hold fast to the faith- *Lord, increase my faith!* (Luke 17:5[85])

"So, in light of this, what do you think of the 'god-sized vacuum in your heart' method?"

"Well, it sounds like competition to me- he's telling me Jesus has a better life for me then I do- a lot of people would disagree- they love their sin and they're quite happy with it (John 3:19, 2 Thes 2:12). It makes Jesus as Savior *optional* in the fact that the person doesn't see the *necessity* of Christ for salvation from hell- they see it as an *alternative* lifestyle."

"Correct. Those who do 'accept' Christ for a better life soon fall away when tribulation (John 16:33), persecution (2 Tim 3:2), temptation (James 1:2), and suffering (1 Peter 4:12-13) strike. They were promised an abundant life and didn't get it, so they fall away. You see, it's not a matter of *happiness*, but of *righteousness*.- Proverbs 10:2 says 'righteousness delivers from death'. Jesus said, 'Unless your righteousness exceeds that of the Pharisees you shall not see the kingdom of God.' (Matthew 5:20). That person witnessing to you is using a better life or happiness as the dangling carrot to salvation instead of your eternity to escape the wrath to come." (Ro 5:9)

"Hmm- that makes sense- I had that experience. I prayed to be a Christian on the promise of a better life, but then afterwards my

---

[85]And the apostles said unto the Lord, Increase our faith.

parents renounced me, my friends taunted me, and I ran into many troubles, so I said 'forget it!'" Andrew replied while pondering it.

"How do you feel towards that person who didn't tell you everything that's involved in being a Christian?"

"Well, I feel they lied to me by not telling me the whole truth. Why were they afraid to not tell me everything?"

"I cannot answer that. Ask them. That still puzzles me today. Think about it. They've just witnessed to someone and they flat out reject Christ. What should that person do then? Shouldn't they at least warn the person of what happens to all who reject Christ? Instead, they've just given that person only half the story- what will happen if they accept Christ; *but not what will happen if they don't*. Wouldn't you think we have an obligation to tell them that? Paul said he did not fail to declare the *whole* counsel of God (Acts 20:27[86])- we should do likewise. Imagine that person who's rejected Christ the day he/she dies. They're standing before God and they find out they're going to hell forever- then they remember the time they were witnessed to and think, *'why didn't they tell me this?!'* I tell you, I certainly don't want to be that Christian."

"Neither would I." Andrew exclaimed in agreement.

"We all know what happens if a person rejects Christ but we find it hard, very hard in fact, to tell that person, 'you'll end up in hell forever'. Oh that stings! Man, that just doesn't sound like our loving God, does it? Before I knew the truth of how to witness I was *never* able to tell that to anyone, and you know why? *I thought it was unreasonable!* Imagine that! I thought God was unreasonable! I knew God was right, but I just couldn't bring myself to say that to a lost person. I thought, 'they'll hate God if I tell them that', or 'I really need to impress upon them God's infinite love for them'. Then I was taught biblical evangelism and God opened my eyes to the truth of the gospel of Jesus Christ! It's the most biblical and complete teaching I've ever heard on witnessing and salvation[87]. Boy, did it

---

86 For I have not shunned to declare to you all the counsel of God.
87 From his book/DVD, *Hell's Best Kept Secret*, available at
    http://www.livingwaters.com/listenwatch.shtml.

open my eyes! (Ps 119:18) I saw godly zeal in the teacher, a meek man, who is eager to see the lost come to Christ. He quoted many godly preachers who lived during times when it was common knowledge among believers that the law much be preached first to prepare the stony heart to prepare it for grace[88].

"After understanding the gospel and salvation from Scripture I found it *completely* reasonable! I remembered the seriousness of my own sin when God saved me and came to know a measure of God's righteousness and holiness that go hand-in-hand with His love. I also chided myself for not finding this out myself. I had a Bible, I could have looked up those verses myself. Now when I get the chance to witness to someone I can eagerly lead them into the truth of their true state before a holy God. I have no fear of asking them the plain result of what would happen to them if they died in their sin and stood before God.

Andrew thought about it and began to see. Then his mind turned

---

88Historically, great preachers knew the importance of the law in converting the soul – consider:

John Wesley said, "*Use 90% law and 10% grace. They'll never come to Christ for grace if they first don't see their need by the law*".

William Tyndale said, "*Expound the law truly, and open the veil of Moses to condemn all flesh and prove all men sinners. And let their wounded consciences drink of Him.*"

Martin Luther said, "*the first duty of the gospel preacher is to declare God's law and show the nature of sin*".

John Wesley's famous sermon, *Sinners in the Hands of an Angry God*, that God used to start a revival, said he was "*saved from the law of sin and death*".

Charles Finney said, "*The severity of the law should be unsparingly applied to the conscience until the sinner's self-righteousness is annihilated, and he stands speechless and condemned before the holy God*". And, "*Failure to use the law is almost certain to result in false hope, the introduction of a false standard of Christian experience, and to fill the church with false converts*".

Charles Spurgeon declared, "*They will never accept Grace until they tremble before a just and holy law*".

to another instance when someone witnessed to him. "Someone once approached me and asked me what I would tell God when I died and stood before Him and He asked me, 'Why should I let you into my heaven?' What about that approach?"

The young man thought it over, "Well, did he convince you of your sin before a holy God?"

"No, she just kept trying to tell me I'd go to hell without turning to Jesus. I had no compelling reason to run to Christ for His free gift of grace (Gal 3:24). It just seemed like she was trying to convince me logically- she was *explaining* the gospel to me instead of *applying* it to me."

"And you never would've run to Christ. The unsaved man *cannot* understand the Bible because he is spiritually dead (2 Cor 2:14). Some evangelize by trying to *explain* salvation to sinners without ever *applying* the law that will convict their conscience by the Holy Spirit that they are *indeed* sinners. They may have an intellectual understanding in their head, but until it becomes a reality in their experience it won't be relevant to them, hence they'll most likely not repent and without repentance it is impossible to be saved."[89] (Eze 18:30-32, Mat 3:3, 9:13, Luke 13:3, Acts 3:19, 17:30, 13:24, 20:21)

Andrew was beginning to see. "There were other times. One time a Christian who was my next door neighbor in my apartment building gave me the Bridge tract. I read it but didn't understand it or consider it relevant since it didn't apply personally to me- it was just another 'theory' of one person's belief on life. I never gave it another thought.

Andrew shook his head as he recalled another instance. "Another time I was waiting in line at my favorite bookstore once and a guy in front of me convinced a girl to have Jesus as a friend and in doing so that made her a Christian. At least she seemed happy about it.

"I later learned that the cashier there was a believer who tried to

---

89 Billy Graham agrees- "If you have not repented, you will not see the inside of the kingdom of God." *The Evidence Bible*, [Bridge-Logos Publishers] pg 418.

witness Christ by her lifestyle- to let people see Jesus in her, but I was lost in darkness and couldn't discern spiritual things so there was no way I'd ever get it that she was a Christian showing God's love to me unless she actually spoke to me and told me.

"I knew two Christians at a job I had years ago that definitely shined the light of Jesus to me, yet they never spoke to me and I erroneously assumed they were 'mightier than thou' because they never hung out with the rest of us or talked about things we did- they had the attitude that they were 'better than the rest of us'. I was mistaken but how would I know that?

"I've had quite a few debates with Christians over the years regarding various forms of evidence God has given us as proof of His existence- the historical accounts that back up the gospels, science, archeology, etc. but I could always defend myself intellectually with the faulty facts I had learned and believed to be true. When someone did get close to telling me the truth it was like I didn't want to really hear it or believe it (2 Tim 4:3-4[90]) so I pretty much ignored it and wouldn't consider it later- I would just harden myself with the 'truth' I knew in order to preserve my sinful lifestyle."

The young man considered what Andrew had said. "So in all these instances what do you think the difference was?"

Andrew thought about it and replied, "Well, they approached me either *intellectually* or *emotionally* trying to *convince* me of what *they believed to be true*. They would say, 'here's what I believe; it's true, so you better believe it or else'. At first I wondered if what they said was true. In my pursuit of life and truth I searched and came up with different answers. I arrived at a different belief, and it always seemed to be a battle between their beliefs and mine. Because of my curiosity and time spent dwelling and thinking over these things I was much better prepared to win the debate."

The young man thought it over and asked, "What would you

90For the time will come when they will not endure sound doctrine; but after their own lusts shall they heap to themselves teachers, having itching ears; And they shall turn away *their* ears from the truth, and shall be turned unto fables.

think of a policeman who pulls you over on the highway and never tells you what law you broke and just gives you a ticket? What would you think of a doctor who diagnoses your ailment and prescribes medicine and tries to persuade you to have surgery without informing you of the illness? What would you think of a Christian who witnesses and tells you that you need to repent and trust Jesus Christ as Savior if they fail to give you the law that you might know why you need Him?"

"I would be offended or stumble. Offended because they claimed that something was true when I didn't believe it. I would then stumble over it because it wouldn't make sense to me."

"And why shouldn't you feel offended? They never told you why. They assumed the duty of convincing you of the truth and then convicting you of the necessity of doing something about it instead of just being witnesses (John 9:25[91]) and let the Holy Spirit convince and convict you through your God-given conscience."

"Ah, I see now!" Andrew exclaimed with joy, "It's not my job to *convince* them; only to *witness* to them!"

"Exactly! Remember the blind man Jesus healed in John chapter nine? When asked of the Pharisees for an explanation he replied, '...I do not know; One thing I know; I was blind and now I see.' (John 9:25) Our job is to *tell* them. It's God's job to *convince* and *convict* them.

Andrew shook his head. "It seems so complicated- I mean there's so many false things people believe that keep them from coming to the truth that they need Christ- how can one ever learn enough to overcome all their years of wrong thinking?"

"You simply preach the gospel to them- is it relevant what 'wrong' things they know? Is it relevant to know where they are in life? The issue is *sin*, and *only* sin: it's not about the troubles in their life; it's not about their lifestyle or sexual orientation- or their childhood or parents. You don't have to wait until their life falls apart in order for

---

91   Whether he be a sinner *or no*, I know not: one thing I know, that, whereas I was blind, now I see.

them to listen to God; nor do you have gain their trust before you can give them the gospel. It's not about *how* they fell into sin; but that they are *by nature* sinners. No matter what's going on in their life, they're sinners and they *need* Christ. *We don't need to understand them; they need to understand God.* And God has given us the honor and duty to give the lost the gospel.

We really don't need to know them or understand them, nor do we need not know all about the sin or false religions they're caught up in. Not once in the Bible does God tell us to learn about the ways of the world or about other false religions before we can witness. In fact, He tells us the opposite, 'be ye separated from the world' and 'you were once in darkness; but now you are children of light in the Lord- walk in light' (1 John 2:15-16, Eph 5:8). Paul agreed, saying he needed to know nothing else but 'Christ crucified' (1 Cor 2:2[92])"

Andrew's gaze told the young man that he was thinking it over. Andrew then asked, "So what is the gospel?"

"Good question. Can you say what the gospel is in a sentence or two? Do you know of a passage that clearly defines the gospel and summarizes it?"

"Not off hand," Andrew replied. He was a new believer and although he knew portions he hadn't read the entire Bible so he couldn't say for sure. "Obviously the four gospels, plus other areas."

"Right, but if we had to boil it down, what would you say? Remember, we need the essence of it to know what to say when we witness. We haven't got all day- in fact, we may have just a few minutes with them."

"Uh, Jesus came to die so we could be with Him forever?"

"Right, that's direct, but kind of general."

"Yeah, I guess it is."

"We know the goal is salvation that the lost person may become a Christian, so what is salvation?"

---

92 For I determined **not to know anything among you**, save Jesus Christ, and him crucified.

"Conversion of the soul- the person is spiritually dead due to sin and he must be born again by God."

"Right- salvation is conversion of the soul. The Holy Spirit regenerates them (Titus 3:5), God forgives their sin (Ro 4:7), justifies them (Ro 8:29-30), redeems them (Gal 4:5), and adopts them as a child (Eph 1:15).

OK, what does God want us to use to bring about conversion?"

"I don't know."

"The law- the Ten Commandments. Psalm 19:7 says The law of the LORD is perfect, converting the soul. This is how God wants us to show the lost that they are sinners. By the law a person knows sin (Ro 7:7). If a police officer pulls you over what's the first thing you ask him- 'what have I done wrong?' You want to know what law you've broken. The police officer tells you and you say to yourself, 'OK, I *did* break the law' and you become convinced of it. But then often times you try to weasel out of the fine. It's the same with the Ten Commandments, When we ask another if he's broken any of the them he'll have to answer yes because God gave him a conscience that he might know sin. Now, he may have hardened his heart or seared his conscience to the point of not knowing it (1 Tim 4:2), but that is his responsibility, not ours. So leave that to God. Our duty is to use the law that is like a mirror that shines upon a person to reveal his sinful state.

"Paul writes in Romans that without the law, he did not know he was a sinner- in fact, without the law there is no sin! (Ro 4:15) *This is profound!* If there was no law there would be no sin, because we could never know we are sinners unless God revealed it to us! Indeed, sin is defined as *transgression of the law* (1 John 3:4). The law applies to everyone and it is through the preaching of the law that the Holy Spirit can bring conviction of sin to the hearer leading to godly sorrow that works repentance.

"We can show this from the story of the woman caught in adultery in John chapter eight. The scribes and Pharisees brought a woman caught in adultery and asked Jesus His opinion, hoping to accuse Him. Jesus wrote in the sand and said, 'He that is without sin among you, let him first cast a stone at her,' and then wrote in the sand again. When they read what He wrote they walked away, one by one, leaving no one to accuse her. Jesus likewise turned to her and said, 'neither do I accuse you. Go and sin no more.'

Now, many have conjectured over the ages what He wrote. We aren't given the actual words but we can surmise the words from verse 9- And they which heard *it*, **being convicted by *their own* conscience**, went out one by one, beginning at the eldest, *even* unto the last: and Jesus was left alone, and the woman standing in the midst (KJV, emphasis added). What clues do we have here? Each person was *convicted* of personal sin in their lives; second, they were convicted *by their conscience*. By what we have discovered previously we know it is God's law that convicts us of sin. Since everyone walked away and were unwilling to condemn her with a stone we can say that every person is convicted of their sinful state by the law. Therefore Jesus most likely wrote one, some, or all of the Ten Commandments in the sand."

Sound Doctrine

Holding fast the faithful word as he hath been taught,
that he may be able by sound doctrine both to exhort and to convince the
gainsayers. -- Titus 1:9

Andrew sat quietly, absorbing the depths of God's word. "That's stupendous! I can't fathom how simple yet how profound the gospel is! I remember how I used worldly wisdom to defeat everyone who witnessed to me- they didn't know the true power of the law! They hadn't used the law which would've stopped my mouth and made me run to the Savior!"

The young man nodded in agreement and continued, "On top of all that Paul writes that the law also brought about the *seriousness* of sin- the utter truth of our sinful state and the ramifications of that before a holy God. Timothy writes that the law is good because it is the means God uses to show us that we are sinners. Just like doctors use x-rays to show us broken bones, so God's law shows us our sin that we might see our need for Christ.

"Now of course, we must use the law wisely (1 Tim 1:8), and with much gentleness; we speak it gently so as not to accuse the person ourselves- we leave that to the Holy Spirit who brings about conviction. We use it wisely knowing it is the teacher or schoolmaster that makes a person *run* to Christ for salvation (Gal 3:24). The law will stop the mouth of anyone who would rather argue about this or that (Ro 3:19)- he may continue his ranting, but by his conscience he knows he's sinned- his conscience will *accuse* him, leaving him guilty before God (Ro 2:15).

"When we preach the law it's between God and them- we are not the one's trying to convince them; it is not between that person and us- that's why we don't need to gain their trust, or even know them. If that person gives us a few moments and hears the plain, clear, gospel then God will do the rest, for the gospel is the power of God unto salvation (Ro 1:17). Those witnessing who are afraid to or don't want to use the law or tell them about hell might actually be ashamed of the gospel of Jesus Christ (Ro 1:16) since they don't either know it, trust it, or believe it."

"Another time I heard a fire-and-brimstone man preaching the wrath of God telling us we better fear God and repent. That's certainly biblical- God has wrath towards the sinner and fear does make one respect and know God's holiness that our sinful state before Him, right?"

"That's correct, Andrew, but that man forgot one very important thing- he forgot to use the law and *personally apply it* to his listeners that the Holy Spirit might bring conviction of sin by their conscience. Yelling at someone *telling* them they're sinners is completely different than *preaching* the law that shines like a mirror on their conscience to reveal their sinful state. Better to let God tell man he is a sinner than us. The world knows this principle as '*tell* a man something and he might believe it- have him *convince himself* and he'll *know* it's true'. Remember, it's between God and man- not *us* telling *them* that they're sinners.

Andrew shook his head, "Again, that makes sense- the law is the gate or door of the gospel that leads one to salvation."

The young man shook his head, "Right! Start in the natural with the goal of swinging the conversation into spiritual things. Do whatever you can to get the conversation started while relying on the Holy Spirit to guide you into using the law, which is good if used wisely and is custom-made for the sinner. Let the Holy Spirit bring about conviction of sin that God might grant repentance through godly sorrow. Then the sinner will *flee* to Christ for salvation!

"This is the approach that Jesus used. In Luke 18:18-27 a proud, self-righteous man came to Jesus asking what he could do to gain eternal life. Imagine someone coming up to you today asking you, 'what can I do to go to heaven?' I think we'd fall over from shock! We'd all love this type of situation. We would simply lead him in the sinner's prayer, right? That not what Jesus did. He gave him the law; five of the Ten Commandments. The man boasted that he had kept the law, but he failed to keep the second greatest commandment- love your neighbor as yourself. Jesus knew this and commanded him to follow it. At this the man became very sorrowful because he loved his wealth. Mark 10:22 says he 'went away grieved'. I guess Jesus blew it, huh? Here comes an excited man *running* to Jesus (Mark 10:17), wanting eternal life and Jesus hammers him with the law, sending him away grieved and sorrowful. Even those watching were surprised, asking, 'who then can be saved?' Mark says the disciples 'were astonished out of measure' (Mark 10:26); Matthew says they were 'exceedingly amazed' (Matt 19:25). Does Jesus' behavior square with today's modern evangelism?

"Or consider when Jesus was with the woman at the well who had five husbands (John 4:7-26[93]). He started in the natural realm in verse 7- He spoke of water that she could relate to; next, He swung the conversation to the spiritual realm in verse 10- He told her about the gift of God, and about living water; next, He brought conviction using the law of God in verses 16-18- He spoke to her conscience by referring to the seventh commandment; finally, Jesus revealed Himself to her in verse 26- He gave her grace by telling her He is the living water that leads to everlasting life."

Andrew began to understand. He dwelt on it for awhile, then considered another time someone witnessed to him. "How about explaining salvation to a lost person using the Roman Road? That's certainly biblical and clearly explains what a sinner is and why he needs Jesus Christ," Andrew wondered.

"You're right- it's all one-hundred percent biblical truth- but the lost person is hearing *an explanation* of salvation instead of being given *an experience* that the Holy Spirit can use to tell them they're a sinner via their conscience (Ro 2:15). When Christians read the Roman Road they think, 'oh, that makes so much sense- and it's

---

93 This paragraph is from *The Evidence Bible*, Ray Comfort, (Bridge-Logos Publishers 2001), pg 326.

explains it so well'. It does, but they forget that the lost person cannot understand Scripture- so trying to explain it to him will make no sense because Scripture is spiritually discerned, and the lost person is spiritually dead and cannot understand spiritual things (1 Cor 2:14). The Christian is trying to witness to their *intellect* instead of to their *conscience* as God commands us to- (1 Tim 1:8-1, Ro 2:15, 3:19, 7:8, Gal 3:24).

"Wow! That makes so much sense! No wonder I could always defeat them intellectually!" Andrew realized. "Even if my arguments weren't sound, I always won because they were trying to battle my intellect instead of appealing to my conscience." Andrew shook his head as he started replacing what he thought was right with Truth. He voiced his thoughts, "to imagine that all the worldly knowledge I've absorbed over these past four years means absolutely nothing when compared to the riches of Christ Jesus and His gospel!" (Col 2:9-10)

The young man smiled as he saw light in Andrew. The two of them thought things over and exalted the Lord God in their minds and hearts.

The day wore on as the two of them continued. Andrew thought about others he heard who had become Christians. "I heard about people getting saved all different ways- they didn't all come to Christ after hearing the Ten Commandments and getting convicted, repenting, and accepting Christ, right? God can certainly use all those situations to bring someone to salvation, correct?"

"Yes, He can, but shouldn't the question be 'am I witnessing according to how God says to do it?' Will God work through untruth? Should we witness in ways not mentioned in the Bible? Why are we not satisfied with the Bible's ways?

"The Bible says salvation is conversion (Matt 18:3) and regeneration of the soul (Titus 3:5); being born again (John 3:3); by grace through faith (Eph 2:8-9); faith comes by the law (Gal 3:24) and the Word of God (Ro 10:17); that the law must be preached (Ro 10:14-15); the law actually *drives* one to Christ (Gal 3:24); people are converted by the law (Ps 19:7); the law is good, holy, and just (Ro 7:12); is made for the sinner (1 Tim 1:9); shows that they are sinners by nature (Ro 7:7); fear of hell drives them to forsake their sinfulness (Pr 16:6, Matt 10:28, Heb 10:31); the Holy Spirit by their conscience (Ro 2:15) will convict them of sin, the need for the righteousness of Christ, and the judgment to come (John16:8); they have godly sorrow leading to repentance (2 Cor 7:10) which God grants (1 Tim 2:25); they repent (Luke 13:3, Acts 20:21, 17:30); they believe by hearing the Word/Bible (Acts 4:4, Eph 1:13, 1 Peter 1:23); and by faith and belief they receive Jesus Christ as Savior and Lord and are soundly converted.

"Do the methods you've seen utilize these truths? Do they rely on God's words verse man's words? Are God's words sufficient? Are God's words outdated that they have become lifeless? Do we need new approaches that are culturally sensitive or politically correct? In short, *have we lost faith in the gospel which is the power of God unto salvation?"*

"I would think the Bible pretty much covers it."

"I would agree. Consider this. Many believe a person's life has to fall apart before they'll turn to Christ. They refuse Christ when they're witnessed to. The believer thinks, 'well, when his life gets terrible, maybe he'll give up his stubbornness and seek God'. Then they wait. Why not give them the law? No waiting is necessary! They can see at once that *their life is in danger of eternal hell* compared to whatever problems life may bring. The Bible says that brings a man to consider the gospel seriously. Look at the rich man who died and was in torment- did he cry that he was innocent? That God was unfair? That he didn't deserve to be there? No, he instantly became a missionary! (Luke 16:19-31[94]).

"Others believe we must understand the sinner that we may be able to relate to them before we can witness. But we already understand them- they're lost without Christ and they'll perish. We understand their sin. We can relate *in the most important way*- that we're

---

94 There was a certain rich man, which was clothed in purple and fine linen, and fared sumptuously every day: And there was a certain beggar named Lazarus, which was laid at his gate, full of sores, And desiring to be fed with the crumbs which fell from the rich man's table: moreover the dogs came and licked his sores. And it came to pass, that the beggar died, and was carried by the angels into Abraham's bosom: the rich man also died, and was buried; And in hell he lift up his eyes, being in torments, and seeth Abraham afar off, and Lazarus in his bosom. And he cried and said, Father Abraham, have mercy on me, and send Lazarus, that he may dip the tip of his finger in water, and cool my tongue; for I am tormented in this flame. But Abraham said, Son, remember that thou in thy lifetime receivedst thy good things, and likewise Lazarus evil things: but now he is comforted, and thou art tormented. And beside all this, between us and you there is a great gulf fixed: so that they which would pass from hence to you cannot; neither can they pass to us, that *would come* from thence. Then he said, I pray thee therefore, father, that thou wouldest send him to my father's house: For I have five brethren; that he may testify unto them, lest they also come into this place of torment. Abraham saith unto him, They have Moses and the prophets; let them hear them. And he said, Nay, father Abraham: but if one went unto them from the dead, they will repent. And he said unto him, If they hear not Moses and the prophets, neither will they be persuaded, though one rose from the dead.

all lost without Christ- we all can empathize with the agony, grief, and loneliness sin brings. *Preaching the gospel to them is the most important thing we can do for the lost.*

"In regards to the testimonies you hear, you may not have heard about them at some point realizing their sin and repenting of it, yet it surely must've happened for Jesus said 'unless you repent you will perish' (Luke 13:3, 5). How do you explain those who make a profession of faith in Christ then fall away? Or those who attend church for awhile but then backslide? Or those who claim, 'I was a Christian once but I'm not now'? How can one know the Lord and then not know the Lord?"

"I don't know..." Andrew replied, curiously wanting to know.

"If one cannot lose their salvation then were those people truly saved in the first place? Could some of those have been the ones that weren't preached the law and never knew godly sorrow and never repented, therefore they never turned from their sin and weren't born again and truly converted? Could a portion of that group be the ones who never obey and serve God out of gratitude because they have never realized the true nature of their sin, hence they can't comprehend God's infinite gift of grace?

"Could a good deal of those be the ones in the statistics that claim 'ninety-five percent of Americans are Christians' yet by looking at our society we see rampant immoral and ungodly movies, books, music, art, and idolatrous love of sports? How could pornographic magazines, web sites, beer commercials, and Sports Illustrated Swimsuit Editions flourish if 'most Americans are Christians'? How could one church promoting a book that sells twenty million copies, while claiming it's bearing fruit making Christians, not result in a noticeable revival in America?

"Look what's happened to our society since the sixties when Satan used men to remove the Ten Commandments from our society- the result is *lawlessness.* The moral bar has been lowered from godliness to debasement; we don't even talk about virtue anymore- instead it's 'family values'. God's holiness and fearful judgment have been replaced by a doting old man who loves everyone regardless of their behavior because it's been deemed by Christians that they don't want to 'sound preachy', or talk about hell.

Andrew hung his head over it all. "What about the statement that 'God hates the sin but loves the sinner'?"

"Where is that in Scripture? Think about it, if God loves the sinner why is *he* cast into hell for eternity if he doesn't come to Christ? Why wouldn't God just cast his *sin* into hell? What's a lost person to conclude if we tell him that? That's his sins go to hell but he doesn't?

Why does God clearly tell us that He has great wrath against the sinner if He doesn't hate the sinner?[95] If that were true then everyone who's ever hated Hitler, murderers, rapists, etc. is wrong for hating the person instead of just the heinous acts they've committed?

Does our court system throw the crime into jail and not the criminal?

Is God unjust towards the sinner because of His hate? No. God is a righteous, perfect, and good judge and by His very nature He must hate sinners and punish them (Is 13:11, 26:21, Joel 2:1-3). Sin originates from the sinner's free will, and they are fully responsible for it.

But praise God! He also loves us with a perfect and unending love (Joel 2:12-13)- so much so that He sent Jesus to die for us while *we were yet sinners!* (Ro 5:8) God takes no pleasure in *any* soul that perishes (Eze 33:11); He wants *all* to come to repentance (2 Peter 3:9). Praise God that He wants His mercy to triumph over His justice! (Jer 18:5-8, Ps 89:14) If that isn't beyond comprehension I don't know what is!

"From a Christian's perspective we see that our forgiven sins are separated from our person and cast away as far as the east is from the west (Ps 103:12) – perhaps that's where this phrase come from.

---

95 Psalm 5:5b ...thou hatest all workers of iniquity. Psalm 7:11b ...God is angry with the wicked every day. Psalm 139:21-22 Do not I hate them, O Lord, that hate thee? And am I not grieved with those that rise up against thee? I hate them with perfect hated; I count them mine enemies.

"God at the same time loves the sinner and has wrath towards him/her. He has wrath towards them as sinners, yet love towards them as expressed in Christ's sacrifice. Mark 3:5 says And when he had looked round about on them with **anger**, being **grieved** for the hardness of their hearts, he saith unto the man, Stretch forth thine hand. And he stretched it out: and his hand was restored whole as the other. Jesus had both *anger* and *grief* towards them *at the same time*. The question becomes which of the two are stronger in bringing a sinner to Christ? Our natural reaction is love, but God clearly says it's fear (Pr 16:6, Ps 90:11). This is due in part to the truth that sinners *love* their sin (2 Tim 3:4) and are *in bondage* to their sin and *do not have the power to break free* (2 Peter 2:19). And God clearly commands us to use the truth of their sinful state in communicating the truth of their need for Christ. John 16:8 says the Holy Spirit will convict sinners of their sin, of their need for righteousness, and the coming Judgment- not God's love, not to fill a god-sized vacuum in their heart, or what a wonderful life He's got planned for them. A person realizes God's infinite love for him/her when they realized what they've been saved from- for *God commended his love toward us, in that, while they were yet sinners, Christ died for them – Romans 5:8.*

Jesus pointed this out in His parable of the two forgiven men. One owed fifty pence, the other five hundred and they both were forgiven their debt. He asked which one was loved more- the answer is the one who had owed more (Luke 7:41-43). Hence, the one who realizes the seriousness of his sin and God's infinite wrath that Jesus suffered certainly rejoices in his great salvation (Heb 2:3). He sings a new song and others are saved when they hear what God has done (Ps 40:2-3)."

Andrew thought it over for a moment. It certainly made sense. Then he thought of something else. "I've been approached by some who used the *4 Spiritual Laws*. That's exactly what every lost person needs to hear!"

"True, but how is it given to the hearer? Does it follow the pattern Jesus used? Is it what God tells us to say? Do we see biblical examples of believers preaching to the lost in that manner?"

"I don't know for sure."

"OK, let's go over them. Here they are- the 4 Spiritual Laws:

> 1.) God LOVES you, and offers a wonderful PLAN for your life.
> 2.) Man is SINFUL and SEPARATED from God. Therefore, he cannot know and experience God's love and plan for his life.
> 3.) Jesus Christ is God's ONLY provision for Man's sin. Through Him you can know and experience God's love and plan for your life.
> 4.) We must individually RECEIVE Jesus Christ as Savior and Lord; then we can know and experience God's love and plan for our lives.[96]

"So what do we have? law one tells the sinner that God has a wonderful plan for his life- we've dealt with this – salvation is not for this life- it's to be redeemed and restored to God our Father; and to escape the wrath to come and avoid an eternal hell by being born-again spiritually.

"Law two is correct however no attempt is made to convince the hearer of this- the Ten Commandments are not applied specifically that the lost person might be convicted in their conscience by the Holy Spirit. What informs and convinces the hearer that the truth/phrase 'Man is SINFUL' applies personally to them? God says only the law can do that (Ro 7:7-8).

"Law three again sidesteps the entire issue of salvation/eternal life and instead promises a grand life- one which every Christian knows is filled with temptation, persecution, tribulation, and spiritual warfare. I personally do not know one believer who has had a single month of 'a wonderful life' without any struggles. Jesus said 'with much

---

96 http://www.greatcom.org/laws/ *The Four Spiritual Laws* was written by Dr. Bill Bright © 1965,1995 Campus Crusade for Christ. All Rights Reserved.

tribulation shall one enter the kingdom of God' (Acts 14:22[97]).

"Law four fails to mention repentance, without which one cannot be saved. Repentance is God-given and comes after one experiences sorrow, which comes from one's guilt before God. Guilt can only come about by conviction, which is brought about by the Holy Spirit only when the law is preached. I cannot find one verse in the Bible that states otherwise- have you?"

Andrew shook his head.

The young man continued, "In conclusion, the entire *4 Spiritual Law* method of evangelism takes a *temporal, this-life* perspective instead of an *eternal, life-to-come* perspective. It dangles a 'wonderful life' theme in front of them instead of the necessity of every person to be redeemed and restored to the Father for all of eternity. This is tragic for the lost person- he is not told what awaits him the moment he dies, instead he is wooed to an attractive life in this world- one which has to compete with his current life of sin which he already loves. Salvation becomes *optional* instead of *mandatory* for his choice is 'Do I want Jesus to run my life?' instead of 'What must I do to be saved?'

"What would the author of these *4 Spiritual Laws* say in reply to this? Well, Bill Bright already has:

> 'In His approximately 42 months of public ministry, there are 33 recorded instances of Jesus speaking about hell. No doubt He warned of hell thousands of times. The Bible refers to hell a total of 167 times. I wonder with what frequency this eternal subject is found in today's pulpits. I confess I have failed in my ministry to declare the reality of hell as often as I have the love of God and the benefits of a personal relationship with Christ. But Jesus spent more of His time warning His listeners of the impending judgment of hell than speaking of the joys of heaven. . . . I have never felt the need to

---

97...exhorting them to continue in the faith, and that we must through much tribulation enter into the kingdom of God.

focus on telling people about hell. However, as a result of a steady decline in morals and spiritual vitality in today's culture and a growing indifference to the afterlife, I have come to realize the need for greater discussion of hell.. . . I have thus come to see that silence, or even benign neglect on these subjects. is disobedience on my part. To be silent on the eternal destinations of souls is to be like a sentry failing to warn his fellow soldiers of impending attack.'[98]

"Ray Comfort writes in his book from which the above was quoted:

'Dr. Bright even took the time to use the law lawfully, by quoting every one of the Ten Commandments, then expounding the law by saying, "Breaking these commandments will take us to hell without the intervening grace and mercy of Jesus Christ" By admitting that "benign neglect on these subjects is disobedience on my part," Dr. Bright revealed his honest humility and his genuine love of the truth.

Please, follow Dr. Bright's example and examine your evangelism methods in light of God's Word. At stake is the eternal salvation of millions of people. You don't need to throw away *The Four Spiritual Laws.* Simply make four important changes. First, don't tell sinners that Jesus will improve their lives with a wonderful plan. Second, don't make the unbiblical mistake of giving the cure before you've convinced them of the disease. Third, take the time to follow in the way of the Master by "opening up" (or explaining) the Ten Commandments. And fourth, faithfully remember to include the terrible realities of Judgment Day and hell'.[99]

---

98 Bill Bright *Heaven and Hell* [NewLife Publications 2002] pages 32, 37, & 48. Also quoted in: Ray Comfort and Kirk Cameron, *The Way of the Master* [Tyndale 2004] pages 78.

99 Ray Comfort and Kirk Cameron, *The Way of the Master* [Tyndale 2004] pages 78-79.

Andrew looked solemnly at the young man, contemplating the ramifications.

"Sad to say, but the key to evangelism that Jesus mentioned in Luke 11:52 has been lost today. We use every means but the law to witness- we use every medium but the plain words of the gospel. We've lost faith in God's word alone to bring sinners to Christ; we're fearful to tell the lost the truth- to mention sin, hell, and God's wrath. So much so that some have become ashamed of the gospel of Jesus Christ (Ro 1:16).

"Well, you certainly are taking the gospel to them!"

"Believers in the first church went everywhere preaching the word one-by-one. (Act 8:4). Peter preached out in the open crowds and went door-to-door (Acts 20:20). Paul went house-to-house as well, 'testifying of repentance towards God and faith towards Christ.' (Acts20:20-21). Jesus commands us to *go* to the sinners- don't wait for them to come to us (Matt 28:20, Mark 16:15). Paul knew the terror of the Lord, and it compelled him to preach the law to the lost (2 Cor 5:11). I do what the Lord enables me to while God brings in the harvest (John 15:5, 1 Cor 3:6-7).

The young man drew close to Andrew and put his hands on his shoulders. He looked straight into his eyes with seriousness of mind, beseeching him, saying, "I urge you, Andrew, continue to be steadfast in God's Word- read it, study it, and live it. Let it replace what the world has taught you with what God has revealed to us. Do this that you might be an example to other believers through your conversations with love in a godly, pure spirit. Give yourself over completely to the things of God that by living for Christ you and others may profit from it. Stay straightway in the precepts and laws of God's truths sprinkled throughout the Bible, for if you do this, you will prove your salvation to yourself and God can save others through you."

He smiled, rose, and departed. Andrew returned the smile knowing the next time he would see the young man would be in paradise.

These things command and teach.

...be thou an example of the believers, in word, in conversation, in charity, in spirit, in faith, in purity.

Till I come, give attendance to reading, to exhortation, to doctrine.

Meditate upon these things; give thyself wholly to them; that thy profiting may appear to all.

Take heed unto thyself, and unto the doctrine; continue in them: for in doing this thou shalt both save thyself, and them that hear thee.

1 Timothy 4:11-13, 15-16

Recommended Reading

Revival's Golden Key
How to Win Souls and Influence People
The Way of the Master
Biblical School of Evangelism
Unless Ye Repent
God doesn't believe in Atheists (formerly titled How to Make an
Atheist Backslide)
Sinners in the Hands of an Angry God

www.ingramcontent.com/pod-product-compliance
Lightning Source LLC
LaVergne TN
LVHW010025070426
835509LV00001B/8